FINDING YOUR IKIGAI

A Real World Practical Guide To Overcoming Adversity And Finding Complete And Lasting Happiness

SANTOSH MENON

www.santoshmenon.org

Every morning in Africa, a gazelle wakes up. It knows that it must outrun the fastest lion, or it will be eaten. Every morning in Africa, a lion wakes up. It knows that it must outrun the slowest gazelle or it will starve to death. It doesn't matter whether you are a lion or a gazelle, when the sun comes up, you'd better be running.

Deep inside you lives an impossible dream. A dream longing to come true. Yet something holds you back...perhaps it is indecision or the fear of unknown, perhaps friends, the past mistakes or something you really can't pin down.

The first key victory you must win is, over yourself. Stay out of your own way. Find your Ikigai (purpose in life) and work towards your dreams.

This book is dedicated to all the "Doers" of the world, who will not say "What an inspiring set of ideas" BUT say " I will do something and be happy in life, whatever it takes."

Contents

This book is dedicated to :

My Parents.

AND

To the three wonderful girls in my life:

Akanksha: My wife, and a constant pillar of support in my life, who kept on pushing me to write this book. Thank you for putting up with me over the years and believing in me.

Shubhangi: For being my reality check as to where lie my limits. You are awesome and inspiring.

Avika : Thank you for keeping me laughing every day and just being you.

KAIZEN-SHARPEN YOUR AXE DAILY

There once lived in a village a woodcutter, who used to make his ends meet by cutting wood daily from the forest and selling it in the marketplace. He used to wake up early, go to the forest with his axe, fell as many trees as he can, cut the trees and make it into small logs and carry it to the market by evening, sell the wood, and on the way back, buy things for his family. This was his daily routine for the last 20 years. He was known in the market as the best woodcutter in town.

One evening while the woodcutter was returning home after a hard day's work, he saw a crowd at the center of the marketplace. He went closer to see what was happening, and he saw the Kings' messenger making an announcement. The messenger was announcing that the king had decided to hold a contest for woodcutters. He said that whoever cuts a hundred trees in a single day will be eligible for hundred gold mohurs (Gold coins) as a reward. He also said that the contest was to commence the next day and was in force for four days from tomorrow.

The woodcutter was very excited and happy on hearing this, as he was confident that he will be able to achieve this feat easily as he had cut 100 trees many times before. He went home very happy that day and narrated about what he heard in the marketplace, about the contest, to his wife, telling her that he plans to go to the forest a little earlier the next day. He said that he planned to wake up early and hence he needs her help to prepare breakfast and lunch a little earlier. His wife was also thrilled and agreed to help him by preparing the food early for him to carry to the jungle.

The next morning, the woodcutter got up earlier than his routine, got fresh, and walked off to the forest. His wife had also gotten up early and made breakfast and lunch for him. As soon as he reached the forest, he started felling down trees with great vigor as he wanted to hit the hundred tree mark as soon as possible. He took short breaks for his breakfast and lunch, and then restarted his work. As the sun set, he stopped his work and counted the number of trees he had felled. It came to ninety. He was a little disappointed that he could not reach the magic number, but vowed to make sure that he hits the target the next day.

He went back to his home and told the same to his wife. His wife was happy that he was able to reach so close, and encouraged him that he will for sure hit the target the next day.

The next day the woodcutter woke up early and marched off to the forest. As he did the previous day, he started felling off trees as soon as he reached the forest, and this time with greater enthusiasm. He took small breaks for breakfast and lunch and continued cutting the trees. As the sun set, he stopped his work and counted the number of trees felled and it was eighty-two. He was surprised and also a little disappointed. He was very hopeful to hit the target that day. With a little heavy heart, he went back home. His wife, when she heard about the same, again encouraged him and said that is okay, and he should not lose hope and believe in his work. She told him to give it one more day's try and give it his all.

The next day the woodcutter again started early and decided he will cut short his breaks and give it his all for the last time. He had taken ample rest at night and he was very confident of meeting his target the third day.

By the end of day three, the count stood at seventy-eight. Now he was a little surprised and disappointed also. He thought something was wrong and decided to meet his guru, (teacher: the person who taught him the art of woodcutting), and find out what is wrong and why he is not able to cut a hundred trees, a feat he had already done so many times in the past.

His guru spoke to him for a long time and asked him in detail as to what he was doing every day when he participated in the contest. The woodcutter explained to him and said he was even waking up early and going to the forest early so that he has more time in his hand, and he also reduced his breaks to give maximum time to cut. He was perplexed as to why despite doing all things possible to meet the target, he was not able to do it. His guru listened to him quietly and then explained as to the reason for his failure.

The woodcutter listened to his guru attentively. The guru asked the woodcutter "When did you last sharpen your axe." The woodcutter thought for a moment and realized that he had forgotten to do this task for a long, long time.

He realized that in his excitement, he had forgotten to sharpen the axe, and every day, he went to cut the trees without doing this basic chore. This was the reason why he was not able to fell hundred trees, despite having done this earlier so many times.

The moral of the story is that we need to keep on upgrading ourselves and sharpening our skills, in whatever field of life we are. Unless we are updated and abreast of what is happening around us, we will be redundant and fall back in the race of life.

THE UNIVERSE HAS YOUR BACK

Ask and it shall be given. Knock and it shall be opened. Believe and it shall be yours to take. These are the timeless wisdom which are universal laws and work every single time, whether you believe in it or not.

These laws are like the laws of the universe. For example like the law of gravity. If you go up a building and jump from there, you will come down, irrespective of who you are, rich or poor, black or white, young or old, man or woman. Just like this irrefutable law of gravity, the law of sow and reap is also working every single time. You cannot plant a neem tree and expect a mango crop. You will get what you sow. If you sow a neem tree, you will get neem only and if you sow a mango tree, you will reap a harvest of mangoes.

The problem is that most of us know these and have heard and read about this multiple times, but have not thought about these seriously, probably because, we have never taken them to be true; which brings us to the topic of belief. It all depends on what you believe.

If you believe that something is true, you will act accordingly and all your thoughts and actions will be directed towards that belief, and if you don't believe, all writings and talks and speeches are a waste. So the first thing to see about yourself is "What are your beliefs." As you believe things to happen, so will it happen. Again, another law of the universe.

From where does belief come. Belief comes from your experiences in life. What you have experienced all through your life through your family, teachers, friends, colleagues, and all, play a great part in how your life unfolded and what your experiences are.

Your life is nothing but a sum total of your experiences. Experiences are controlled or affected by your circumstances to a great extent. To a level, you cannot change your circumstances. You had no choice in selecting your parents, the environment that they lived in, and how they behaved and lived when you were a child.

These circumstances were not in your control and they had a great influence in shaping you as a person. It is from these experiences in life that your beliefs developed.

But the good news is that though you had little influence on your past as you grew up, you can change your beliefs the day you decide. When you realize that your beliefs are a hindrance to your growth and your daily living, you can change them in an instant and redirect the ship of your life to a new and rewarding path. But habits once formed are tough to break and hence it will require great effort from your side, a disciplined effort, to change your beliefs and make a new world.

CHANGE YOUR THOUGHTS- CHANGE YOUR LIFE

The first step to changing your beliefs is by changing your thoughts. Your thoughts affect your beliefs, your beliefs affect your actions, and your actions affect your destiny/life. A human mind has an average of six thousand thoughts a day, and what is amazing is that ninety-five pc of these thoughts are repeated thoughts, which means they are more or less the same thoughts.

Hence, the first step towards changing your life is to change the way you think. If the thoughts you had till now is not helping you, it is high time you change your thoughts. To change your thoughts for the better, you need to know what you are thinking every day, hour, minute, and second. You need to observe your thoughts. Keep a close watch on what your mind thinks every minute.

Once you have a handle on what you are thinking, you need to understand if those thoughts are helping you to achieve what you want in life. The moment you realize that these thoughts are not working for you in any way, you need to discard such thoughts and train your brain to think thoughts that are of benefit to you and which directs you towards your goals. This has to be a deliberate and conscious process, and every time you are faced with such a situation, where you realize that you are having negative thoughts, it is your responsibility to change it immediately and direct your mind to think positive thoughts which are moving you towards your vision of life.

But then as pointed out earlier, the reason why your brain is constantly thinking about negative thoughts is that it has been trained to do so over the years, it has been your habit for all these years.

So, to break that habit one needs to have a conscious and willful effort from one's side, and that will happen only when you realize:

1) What are your habits and thoughts?

2) If these thoughts and habits are actually working against you, and that there is an urgent need to change them.

3) If you are really serious about changing your life and you want to be in control of your life.

Thoughts rule our life. We are on autopilot mode for the most part of our waking day. We are driven by habits that we have developed all the years into our adulthood, and we repeat these thoughts and actions day in and day out. We are ruled by the thoughts that come and go in our mind, and instead of we controlling the mind, the mind is controlling us.

ADAPT OR PERISH

There is a Chinese fable about two monks who were going to the town from their monastery. On the way lay a small stream which they had to cross bare foot. As they were about to cross, one of the monks saw a lady who was blind and was trying to cross the stream. In their monastery, there was a custom that men were not supposed to touch a woman, because as per their tradition, it would make them impure.

The older of the two monks saw that the lady was blind and there was no way she could have crossed the stream. He stood there and thought for a while. The younger monk asked what is he waiting for. The older monk did not utter a word, and moved towards the blind woman and offered to help her cross the stream. In order to do that, he had to lift the woman and then cross the stream with her. He lifted the woman, as the younger monk continued to look at him with a look of contempt. They both crossed the stream, with the older monk carrying the woman. Once they had crossed the stream, the old monk put the woman down and told her that she had crossed the stream. The blind woman thanked and blessed the monk, not knowing who helped her. The two monks walked their way to the market.

Two days passed since the incident and the older monk could see that there was a difference in the behavior of the younger monk towards him, since the day of that incident where they had crossed the stream and the older monk had carried the blind woman and helped her cross the stream. It was the evening of the third day that the younger monk came to him and told him that he wanted to speak to him. The younger monk said that there was something that was troubling his mind, and he wanted to discuss the same with him. The older monk sat down with the younger monk and asked him what was troubling him so much. The younger monk said "Master, I still can't forget that day when you carried that woman and helped her cross the stream. This is against our monastery rule, which says that men are not supposed to touch a woman, as that will make them impure. Can you please let me know why you did the same, knowing very well that this was against our tradition? Of note, is that younger monks in that monastery addressed the senior monks as Master.

The older monk smiled and looked at the younger monk and said "Dear, I carried the woman for maybe 10 minutes, but you have been carrying her for more than 60 hours now." Drop any incident which does not serve you a good purpose and let people decide what is right or wrong, good or bad, for themselves as they are the ones who are going to reap the fruits of their action or inaction. I very well understand that it is against our monastery rules to touch a woman, but what we have to keep in mind here is that the greater rule in our monastery has always been and still continues to be to help a person who is in need, as there is no greater rule or work than serving another fellow being. Had I not helped the woman cross the stream, she would have never been able to cross it and there was a greater chance that she would have met with some mishap as she was blind. Hence, the greater call of helping a person in need overruled the other thought in my mind, and hence I acted accordingly. The younger monk looked at his senior in awe as he was in complete agreement with what the senior monk was saying and he bowed before him and said, "Thank you master for opening my eyes."

MIND AS SERVANT OR MIND AS MASTER

God has gifted us all our faculties including the mind to use them properly and not to be used by them. We should not become slaves of our faculties but rather drive them to do things that are good for us and for the benefit of a larger cause.

Let us take another example of how we can drive our mind and not be driven by it, as happens with many of us in our day-to-day lives. As pointed out earlier, we are on autopilot mode most of the time and we need to get off this mode and be in control of our mind in order to have a life of balance.

It is very much possible to control our mind if we wish to. However, please note that being in the autopilot mode is being in the comfort zone, and for most of us, unless there is a great physical danger or anything that will cause us great damage in terms of our being, we are ok with being in the comfort zone, that is being on autopilot and doing nothing to change our circumstances or the way we live. We cannot expect to have a better life, a more balanced and prosperous and peaceful life unless we are ready to get out of our autopilot or comfort zone and take some action that will move us towards our desired goals and objectives in our lives. Of note is that we need to first ask ourselves, honestly, if we are fine with living the way we are living currently or there is a need to change. The universe always sends us messages in various forms to tell us that there is something not right in our lives and needs to be changed. It's up to us to ignore those messages and continue living the same way, or we take those messages as opportunities for change and do take some concrete action and change things for the better.

For a moment, think of yourselves as eating a ripe mango, and you are enjoying the process. The mango is very sweet and very tasty and you are currently relishing the same. Now shift your thought and think of eating a double sundae ice cream of your choice. Think that you have the best ice cream, the one you love to have, and you are licking at it. How is the feeling? Did you enjoy the ice cream as much as you were enjoying the mango just a minute back?

This is to prove the point that we can direct our minds to do and think what we want at our will. The mind needs to be our servant and not our master. The moment we let the mind control us, we have lost the initiative and the momentum and will be a slave to our old habits and thoughts.

THE WORLD IS OUR TEACHER

We are here to learn lessons and the world is our teacher. When we fail to learn a lesson, we get to take it again...and again. Once we have learned the lesson, we move to the next one... and we never run out of lessons. We reach points in our lives when we are ready for new information.

Until then, something can be staring us in our face but we don't see it. We continuously and deliberately avoid these as they ask uncomfortable questions, and also make us think if what we are doing is right and what should be the course forward.

The new way may be a completely different path, which has got hardships, and which is the path we need to follow if we are to achieve our goals or live our heart's desire.

We wait till the last minute when some catastrophe is about to hit us and then act. Many of the times this is not enough and we may be too late to even act, and then we regret why we did not take action at the right time. The only time most of us ever learn anything is when we get hit over the back of our head. Why? Because it's easier not to change. So we keep doing what we are doing until we are hit by a brick wall.

WHY DO I NEED DISASTERS

Take our health for example. When do we change diets, go for exercise, cut down on carbs and fats? Only when our body is falling apart and when the doctor says if you do not change your lifestyle, you may kill yourself.   Suddenly, we are motivated.

In relationships, when do we usually tell each other how much we care and love: when the marriage is falling apart, when the family unit is threatened.

When do we usually pray: When our life is falling apart! As long as things are normal, at least from our way of looking at things, we are not much concerned, or even believe in prayers. However, once we hit a crisis, we seek God's blessings and pray to him to set things alright.

We learn our biggest lessons when the going gets tough. When do we make life-changing decisions in life? When we are on our knees- after disasters and after we have been kicked in the head. That's when we say to ourselves "I am sick of being broke, tired, being kicked around, and of being mediocre. Let me do something about it and change immediately."

Effective people don't go looking for problems, but when they get smacked in the mouth, they ask themselves - "How do I need to change what I am thinking and what I am doing?" "How can I be better than I am right now?" Losers ignore all warning signs. When the roof falls, they ask, "Why does everything happen to me?"

We are creatures of habit. We continue doing the same thing again and again until we are forced to change.

So, is life a series of painful disasters? Not necessarily. There are numerous examples of how an event that seemed tragic initially turned out to be for the better.

Priya got divorced from her husband Rahul and her life was shattered. She locked herself up in her bedroom for 2 weeks, completely devastated and cut off from the outside world. After 2 weeks, she started calling old friends and came out of her shell, and met new friends. She moved to a new locality and got a new job. Within 6 months, she is happier and more confident and looks back at her past life as a bad dream. She now even considers divorcing Rahul as the best thing that happened to her life.

Ramesh got sacked from his job after working for 15 years with the firm. He had put his blood and sweat into his work, and when he was laid off, he went into depression. For few weeks, he was unable to understand what went wrong and was in complete denial mode. Slowly, he recovered and applied for a new job, which he got, worked harder, and is now in Australia, living the life of his dreams. He looks back at the sacking incident as a blessing in disguise.

WE ALWAYS HAVE A CHOICE

In all situations in life, we have two choices. We can either lament about what happened and immerse ourselves in sorry and self-pity and live in complete denial mode, agonizing the incident and living a miserable life; or we can see the incident as a wakeup call for us to get our house in order and work towards improvement and betterment of life. How we handle such situations will determine the quality of our lives.

Some things are beyond our understanding and explanation. A child born with Autism, another one with AIDS; a devastating flood, or an earthquake wiping off an entire village, does not have any explanation and we end up asking ourselves "Why?" For these things, there does not seem to be an answer, but for a majority of events in our lives, there are answers and we can find some clues- if we search for the same.

We are constantly being presented with lessons, and unless we learn from them, life continues to give us lessons again and again and again. Like it or hate it, it is happening. Take responsibility or claim you are a victim. Fight it or ignore it, it is happening in any case.

Every time your neighbor abused you or you had a fight with your spouse or you lost a job; each incident has a lesson for us to look for and learn our lesson and move on. We are not here to be punished. We are here to be educated. Every event has the potential to transform us, and the bigger the event, more the disastrous it is, the greater the potential to change our thinking and our outcomes from them. Act as if every event has a purpose and your life will have a purpose.

YOU ARE EVERYWHERE YOU GO

Be it a nagging husband or a creepy boss, all have a lesson to teach you, and the only person to change in any case is you. You need to look at things from a different angle and not just wish for the change to happen. It so easy to divorce a husband who is a pain in the butt, but if you continue to think about him and the incident, you have not learnt your lesson. While for all self-justified reasons, you can blame him for the misery you are in, you have to understand that it is your belief about the person on the incident that will either make you dwell in that or liberate from that situation; you are the one to take a call. We chose how we see people and incidents. It is completely upon us to make the change for the better or worse.

The same goes with a creepy boss. As long as you are convinced that he is a creepy person, he will continue to be one. The moment you decide to change your focus on to his good qualities and stop judging him, even empathize a little with the person, the problem will disappear. "How?" you say. Life works in mysterious ways. He can either get transferred to a different department or office, or you may get a promotion and move out, for reasons unknown to you, and his attitude towards you will change and you may find him more reasonable and easy to work with. How does this happen is not for you to look out for and neither is it my job to explain it here. But it happens. That is the truth. When you change, situations and circumstances change. Your outlook towards life and the various challenges it throws at you will determine your outcomes. Change your response and you will see a changed outcome.

Maybe if I go to a new city, things will change. Maybe if I change my job, it will be better for me. Wrong. Usually, the best place to make a new start is the place you are in currently.

Take Peter for example. He owes money to half the neighborhood and people are always at his door or calling him asking for their money. Peter is completely frustrated and angry at his situation and is thinking about changing his city. What Peter misses is that wherever he goes, he takes his thoughts, his attitude, and his habit patterns with him. He changes his city and will attract the same situation, as he has not changed his way of living, and will end up having another set of angry creditors. Lessons chase us wherever we go. It is not the city or the place or the climate that determines how happy or how miserable we are in a given situation. It is our outlook towards life and the principles we live by that determine our living.

Going to holy places or monasteries will not help us find the meaning of life or a solution to our problems. We need to find solutions within ourselves, wherever we are, and with whatever we have.

The only way to beat our fears and win over our challenges is by facing them. We need to understand that all incidents have a lesson to teach us, and we need to take the lesson from it and move forward. You attract more what you resist. If being in debt is your biggest problem, you will attract more of it. If loneliness is your biggest fear, you will attract that. It's life's way of encouraging us to grow.

CAUSE AND EFFECT

We are each a cause. Our thoughts attract and create the circumstances that we find ourselves in. As we change, we attract different circumstances. Unless we learn a lesson from the event, we continue to keep on getting the same event in different forms. We get hit by little pebbles - as a kind of warning. When we ignore the pebbles, we get hit by a brick, ignore the brick, and we get wiped out by a boulder. If we are honest we can say where we have ignored the warning signs; and work toward immediate repair, before it is too late. We ignore all these warning signs and then we have the nerve to say "Why me?"

It's easier to get philosophical about other people's pain and be judgmental and pass remarks on other's problems.

When Sheela gets divorced and decides to live separately and start a life on her own, and she does succeed in carving a niche for herself in life, we can hear comments like "Whatever happened for her was for her good. See, she is so happy now and so successful." OR, When Ram meets with an accident and he loses his job, and struggles to make both ends meet for quite some time, then starts his own small firm and hits big and gets successful, comments like, "It was good for him. See where he is today."

What is however surprising is that when these same challenges come our way, we are not so enthusiastic about the same and wish we had something easier to handle. We end up saying "Lord why this. Give me a more convenient challenge." Unfortunately, real challenges are not convenient.

ITS NOT WHAT HAPPENS, ITS HOW WE RESPOND

If only I could have quality people in my life is another great wish that people have. We need to understand that every single person we encounter in our life, comes into our life for a reason and they serve a purpose, it is for us to identify the lesson and learn from it and move ahead.   If you have a husband who is not very organized and always keeps socks and clothes in a messy way, while you are a very organized person, you need to understand that there is a lesson for you.

If you have a nagging wife who always complains about every single thing that you do and you are at loggerheads at all times with your wife, you need to understand that there is a lesson for you. If you think that divorcing her or him is the solution, you are sadly mistaken. In both these cases, your partner is testing your limits and letting you know where your limits are. You need to learn how to handle such people and situations so that when faced with a tougher situation or person, you are well equipped to handle the same.

Every person who walks into your life is a teacher...even if they drive you nuts.

When does life get simpler? It doesn't, but we can learn how to handle it better. One of the main reasons why life does not get simpler is that we go out looking for complications in life. Sounds funny, but that is a fact. One EMI or loan gets over, and we go for another one. A bigger house, a bigger car...and the list goes on. We end up buying things with money that we don't have to impress people we don't like and get into something called the debt trap. And we expect our lives to be simpler.

Reflect on your life and you will find a reason why you took the path you did. Reflect on the people who came into your lives including your parents, your teachers, your friends, and all who have touched your life at one point or other and you will realize they all taught you a lesson.

The universe is a patient teacher. Watch the signals and life runs relatively smoothly. Ignore them, and wham! You get a new lesson to learn and then a new one and so on. The sooner you learn the lesson, the better your life will be.

Garbage in, garbage out. What you have been feeding your mind all these years determines the results you are having now. If nothing good is happening in your life, look at what you have been putting in. When you take a good look at your life and acknowledge that you are responsible for what you have and what you don't have and where you are currently in your life, you cease to be a victim. You understand that you are responsible for everything that has happened in your life till date. Be honest and you can list out almost everything that has happened to you and also see how you have helped to create it. Nothing in your life has happened or will happen without your permission and knowledge. Everything that has happened to you, has been brought into your life, knowingly or unknowingly, by you and you are one hundred percent responsible for the same. The day you realize this and are ready to accept and change, your life will take a completely new turn and things will begin to look up and be better as you work consciously towards a better life for yourself. The most important thing is to see that, acknowledge that, and also to accept that you are the cause and take full responsibility for the same.

THE LAW OF THE SEED

You reap your harvest after you do the work. You dig the soil, plant the seed, water the seed, protect it from rain and sun and then wait (Patience). It is then that you harvest. It is called the law of sow and reap.

Effort + Patience= Result

You plant today and you harvest later. It simply means that it takes time for your crop to be ready for harvest and you cannot expect immediate results. You can neither wish for the result before sowing. Bob says "If only I had that promotion, I will stop sleeping at my job." It never happens that way. "Pay me more and I will stop being sick." We need to understand that there is no reversing the process. We need to put the effort first and then ask for the result.

Another law of sowing is: You plant some and you get some. You cannot expect to get the same amount back. When you sow the seeds, some are eaten by birds, some decay, some are blown away by the wind and you get the remaining. If you plant a dozen, you don't get a dozen back. However, if you nurture the seeds well and take care of them through the seasons, you may reap a much richer harvest.

You have to go through a lot of friends to find a few good real friendships. You need to go through many candidates who have applied for a particular job to select the most suitable candidate. This law of selection applies in many aspects of life.

AS YOU GET BETTER, THE GAME GETS BIGGER

Life is a gradual progression and you need to work to get to the next level. You cannot expect to go to the next level and work to meet the requirements. You need to upgrade yourself first before you move to the next level.

"I wish I had a team of thirty team members and I would have beaten all records of Insurance sales." No, it does not happen that way. What do you do when you have a smaller team of two is what will determine when you will have a team of thirty, and what would be your success rate at that level. As they say "morning shows the day," what you do when numbers are small will determine if you will have bigger numbers and your subsequent success. What you do with what you have will determine how much more you will have. One thing leads to another. Start small and then see things grow. Don't wonder at someone leading your dream life and think how did he or she get there or that they were luckier than you. Don't think how did life become so sweet for them. They made a small start somewhere. And that small start led to something else and that led to something else which finally grew to this size. It has always been a progressive realization for every single person.

Start with whatever you have. Give it your best shot to whatever is in front of you, and opportunity will begin to find you. It's called developing a reputation. It's called "one thing leads to another."

The universe rewards efforts and not excuses.

THE FROG PRINCIPLE

There is an oft-quoted story about a frog and a bucket of water. Take a healthy and happy frog and put it in a bucket of hot water. The frog will immediately jump out of the water as it feels the heat is hard for it to bear.

Take the same frog or any of his relatives and put him in a bucket of cold water. Put the bucket on a stove and slowly heat the bucket. The frog will enjoy the cold water and will soon be enjoying warm water too. However, unless he realizes it early, we will soon have cooked frog.

Moral of the story: Life happens gradually. Like the frog, we can be fooled, and suddenly it is too late. We need to be aware of what is happening. Things happen gradually and reach a stage that is out of control. We gradually gain weight, overspend, have a bad relationship which leads to divorce. We ignore when things are small and suddenly cry foul when they go out of hands. Life is accumulative. One thing adds to another- like the drops of water that wear away the rock. The frog principle is telling us to watch the trends. Every day we need to ask ourselves: "Where am I heading? Am I fitter, healthier, happier than I was last year?" If not, we need to change what we are doing. There is no standing still in life. We either move forward or fall behind. There is nothing called status quo in life.

SELF-DISCIPLINE

Self-discipline makes all the difference. If there is one thing that separates the haves from the have nots, the successful from the not-so-successful, the happy from the not-so-happy, it is discipline.

Have the discipline to do the little things you don't like and you can spend your life doing the big things which you do like.

Life is a tradeoff between instant pleasure and long-term reward. Studying instead of TV leads to a big thing- better qualification; three sessions a week at the gym- leads to a big thing, a healthier life.

The key to self-discipline is not an iron will but the knowing of WHY you want something. When you know why you want to get out of debt, you will save automatically, when you know why you want to improve your qualification, you will study more.

It is these WHYs that will push us to be more self-disciplined and show us direction as to where we need to head to improve our life. Discipline enforced by some person or circumstance is not very encouraging and that will not last long.

People who are not self-disciplined often get it from outside. They often get into a job in which they take orders from their superiors or bosses.

With discipline comes order. Everything about nature is orderly. There is order in every single aspect of nature, except humans. That is something we need to cultivate and develop and does not come naturally to us. Nature keeps what is essential and discards the rest. That is called organization.

After discipline, one needs to focus on being orderly as that makes all work a lot more easier. Your desk is in a mess and you want everything to happen on time. It never happens that way.

Nothing blooms out of a mess. Organize your life and things will be better. Clean up the mess that is around you. They say "As within, so without" which means that if you have an unorganized and messy external, it is a reflection of your internal world. Your environment is a direct reflection of the disorderliness and mess that your life is in.

NO EFFORT IS WASTED

The Chinese bamboo tree. They say if you plant a Chinese bamboo tree and water it daily, you will see nothing coming out of the ground for years together. Even if you continue to water it daily for 5 years, nothing happens. One need not get disappointed and continue watering and taking care of the seed where they have planted. Then suddenly after 5 years, the shoot springs and within a year it grows to be a huge tree. The question is whether the tree grew so big in one year or six years. To draw a corollary, we should have faith in our efforts and continue doing the work which we are doing. We should not get disheartened or discouraged if we don't see the results we expect. We need to work in faith and work to our full potential till we start seeing results, and we will. No effort in this world goes waste. Every effort that you put with your whole heart and sincerity yields results. It is a law of the universe and it works - every single time. You get rewarded in proportion to the quantum of effort that you put in. The harder you work, the better is the reward.

One word of caution here is that we need to understand that everything in life happens in waves, which means in bunches. Family crisis, wedding invitations, car repairs - all happen in bunches and hence we should be mindful of that and be ready for the same. It makes our lives easier if we are aware of what is coming and make us better prepared for any eventuality.

CHANGE IS THE ONLY CONSTANT

Change is the only constant; the sooner we accept this, the easier it will be for us to navigate through the challenges of life. What is true and applicable today may not be true or applicable a few years from now. At the pace at which the world and technology are changing our lives, we cannot even think of things changing drastically over years, they may change in months or even in weeks.

Jobs that were in very much relevance 10 years ago have either become obsolete or has become redundant and companies have shunned it for better technology or better ways to do it. We had studied in high school biology on the laws of natural selection- adapting to change. If a green bug does not change its color in a brown field, it is in big trouble. There is no point complaining "The field should be green, it has always been like that."

There is a big lesson that we need to learn there in our biology classes. Change and adapt or perish. The law is brutal- adapt or disappear. Something like what happened to dinosaurs in the old ages. They were not able to adapt to changing climatic conditions of the earth and hence perished.

In the corporate world, things change, and the sooner we are able to adapt to new technology or process, the better are our chances of survival. If we are in no mood to adapt ourselves to the rapidly changing world, we will become redundant and will be out of a job.

In 1927, Harry Warner at Warner Brothers Pictures said "Who the hell wants to hear actors talk?"

In 1943, Thomas Watson, chairman of IBM said "I think there is a world market for 5 computers."

In a nutshell, happy people don't just accept change; they embrace it. They are the ones who ask "Why should my next 5 years be the same as the last 5?"

CHANGE THE WAY YOU LOOK AT THINGS AND THE THINGS YOU LOOK AT WILL CHANGE

Our limiting beliefs about self are the traitors and make us live the lesser lives that we live.

There was a big caravan of merchants moving along the Thar desert with their herd of camels and were crossing the desert to do trade in the city on the other side of the desert.

They had to spend days and nights in the huge desert and movement along the desert was slowed down as the camels are not very swift animals. This caravan would travel the whole day and stop in the evening, tie their camels near the tents on a peg, give them fodder and water and call it a day for the rest of the night. They would restart their journey the next day morning. The camels would remain tied to the peg the whole night, ready for the journey the next day.

One day, after traveling for the whole day, as the sun came down, the merchants decided to stop near an oasis. They had the caravan stop and asked the caretakers to tie the camels so that they could rest. There were a total of thirty six camels as part of this journey. As the caretakers settled down and were tying the camels near the tent, one of them found out that one rope was missing to tie one of the camels. They searched everywhere and the rope was not to be found.

This was a serious issue as the camels need to be tied at night or they will wander away from the group. The caretaker in charge of that camel went to the head merchant, who was a wise man, and told him the problem. The merchant thought for a while and told the caretaker to take the camel near the peg where it was supposed to be tied, pretend as if he is tying a rope to the peg, move his hands in a circle around the peg and then leave it. The merchant said this will solve the problem.

The caretaker was surprised but he had no choice but to listen to the head merchant. He did exactly as was advised. And then he went a little distance, sat there, and watched what the camel did. He observed that the camel came near the peg, circled it few times, and sat near the peg as if he has been tied there.

To his surprise, when he woke up in the morning, he found the camel sitting at the same place and not having moved even an inch. As the morning progressed, they were all ready to pack and move to the next destination. He made the camel stand up and tried to have the camel move. To his surprise, the camel did not move. It stood its ground and whatever the caretaker did, the camel stood there as if it is still tied to the peg.

When all efforts to move the camel failed, the caretaker ran to the head merchant and narrated the whole story. He said the camel is refusing to move and all are ready to move ahead. The head merchant smiled and asked the caretaker to go near the camel and the peg and reverse circle his hands around the peg as if he is untying the rope that held the camel the whole night. He said once you do this, the camel will move.

The caretaker was perplexed but he had to listen to the merchant. He went back and did exactly what the head merchant had told him to do. The moment he moved his hands in an anticlockwise direction as if he was untying the camel, the camel started moving ahead. The caretaker was surprised and amused at the same time.

Out of curiosity, this caretaker went to the head of the merchants and asked him what had happened and why the camel behaved such. The head of the merchants told the caretaker that the camel saw that he had tied it to the pole and believed that the tying was real and indeed the camel could not move. In the morning, he still was in the same state believing that he is tied to the peg. As the caretaker did not untie the rope (figuratively), the camel continued to believe that it is tied and hence refused to move.

This is the same case with we humans. Right from our childhood, with all good intentions, whatever our parents, teachers, friends told us, we grew up believing them to be true. Statements like: Money doesn't grow on trees; you will amount to nothing when you grow up; you are hopeless in mathematics; you sing like a duck; it is so difficult to earn money; are some of the most common statements that we hear as a child and we grow up believing them to be true.

As these statements come from people in authority like our parents and teachers; whom we completely trust and believe in, we grow up believing them to be true and continue that same belief throughout our lifetime. We create our own glass cage and believe that is our reality. We try our whole life to fit into that image that has been built of us.

DROP THE "I"

What is your story? What labels you have attached yourself with? I am a doctor. I am a teacher. I am a software engineer. These are the various labels that we have attached ourselves to and we try to fit ourselves to this tag. Wherever we go, whatever we do, we try to conform to these tags and live and behave to reflect these norms. Our entire life is made to reflect how each of these tags make us live, have, and behave. This is called trying to fit into the story, and this is exactly what makes our lives miserable.

Here is the truth. YOU ARE NOT YOUR STORY AND NOBODY CARES ANYWAY. You don't belong to a category or fit in a box. You are a human being having a series of experiences. When you quit dragging a story around, you never have to look the part.

I AM A VERY IMPORTANT PERSON- PEOPLE SHOULD TREAT ME ACCORDINGLY! Some people are obsessed with the fact that others should recognize them as to how rich they are, how educated they are, and how many degrees they have got. The flip side of this feeling is that while you demand that other people think that you are important, you have given the control of your happiness in their hands. Every time this does not happen, you feel low and beat yourself up. The moment you forget the need to feel important and the need to have others feel your importance, you relax. You live in a much more happier space.

One needs to get rid of all the If's and But's in life. If I was young.... If I was rich..... If I was slim.... There is only one way to live, and that is to be learning, and loving what you do, right up to the last minute. Ask yourself, " What would I do if I had no story?"

Any belief that keeps you poor and miserable and does not allow you to grow fully as an individual, shun all such beliefs. Forget about being importat - it's too stressful. The less you demand appreciation from others, the more you get.

DROP:

1. People should return favors.
2. People should praise me.
3. People should be more considerate.
4. People should be grateful

Don't try to change people, change your beliefs. As long as you do not expect people to behave in a particular fashion- you will have peace of mind.

YOUR BELIEFS DETERMINE YOUR QUALITY OF LIFE

Whatever thoughts are causing you pain, they are only thoughts and thoughts can be changed.

Your bank balance will always match your belief systems. When your self-image does not fit your bank balance, it's easier to change your bank balance- it's our thoughts that control our lives and not external factors.

To have something in life, you need to be comfortable with it. To make money, and keep it, you must be comfortable with money.

If your thoughts are of jealousy when you see a rich person, you are sending a message to the universe that you are not comfortable with money. When you see a nice car or a nice house and wonder how that person got it or feel jealous about that person, you again are not sending the right signals out.

You NEED to be comfortable with all this before you manifest it in your life. Feel prosperous to attract prosperity. Prosperity is not a money thing- it is a lifestyle thing.

For the world to treat you well, you have to treat yourself well. Self-love precedes all other love in the world. If you have no self-love or pride in who you are as a person, no one else can give it to you. Events will unfold according to your expectations. The minute you change your beliefs about your situation, your different thoughts will attract different people and new opportunities.

Most people through their lives are driven by their own beliefs and never stop to check if their beliefs are working in their favor or against them. They never think about alternate solutions- change belief.

Our belief and expectation that people should behave in a certain way is the cause of most agony in our relationship with other people. The moment we drop this expectation of other people to do or behave in a certain manner, we enter a more peaceful space with all.

We will see others in a new light, and it is not late before we realize that our old beliefs and patterns of thoughts about other people have resulted in so many heartburns and loss of good friendships or relationships.

Next time you are upset or angry, remember it is not people who make you angry, it's your own beliefs. Consider alternate solutions. Have the courage to think unfamiliar. Whatever thoughts cause pain-change them- after all they are thoughts.

MY JOB SUCKS

Stop blaming your job for your problems. Remember, it is something you have chosen to do and understand that your attitude towards your job will determine how you feel towards it. If you think your job is a drag, it will turn out to be so, and if you think your job is interesting, so will it be.

Change your thought to "Work is Fun!" and see the magic. Remember it is always your thoughts and it is in your hands to change it.

RELATIONSHIP WITH MONEY

Prosperity involves you running your mind regardless of what your neighbors and the papers say. Even if you are on a fixed salary, your prosperity will be determined by, not by the money you make, but what you believe about money.

Just to prove the point, take seven people in an organization at the same designation and pay scale. In the same group, you will find some people with assets and living well and some living their lives deep in debt.

The difference is not in the money that they make but what they believe about money. If you have not got the money that you want or if you are feeling like you are losing it, there is a reason for the same-and it's not due to some external factor-it is an inside thing.

Lottery winners are a classic example of how one's belief systems determine their prosperity. People think money will solve their problems. Yet most people who win lotteries are broke two years down the line. This is because the belief system that I am broke always proves to be true even after winning the lottery.

A man in Australia won the lottery twice and lost it all within two years of winning. Your relationship with money will determine if you are prosperous or not.

Some people like to be broke and they never ask the obvious question as to why they are broke. They seem to be happy in that space which is their comfort zone as they believe that there are advantages to being broke.

The need for people to get the sympathy of others, not discipline themselves, blame it all on others- the people, the government, are some of the advantages of being broke and which some people like to dwell in. It is this attitude towards life and money that keep some people broke.

Most people are embarrassed about money. They may be living on a meager income, but offer them some money and they will hesitate to the core as if they don't like money. Some feel insulted with such gestures and react defensively. I don't need your money, I am fine.

Some of us have trouble even talking about money, as though money is a bad thing to talk about. We lend money to someone and then don't know how to ask for it back. We talk around the topic with the person and move round and round but don't come to the point about asking the person to give the money back. We say everything but "Can you give my money back?"

It is the law that is working at all times in our lives. If you are uneasy in a job or uneasy in a relationship, sooner or later you will part company. The same goes for money. If you are nervous even talking about it, if money doesn't sit with you well, you will soon part with money too. It's not a conscious thing- it's an unconscious thing. Things we are awkward with, we part or avoid.   In order to have something in life and keep it, you need to be comfortable with it.

IF I HAVE PLENTY- OTHERS WILL GO WITHOUT

This is another common myth that people live by, and we too hear very often. One needs to understand that the more you have, the more you will get.

The universe is full of abundance in everything. It has enough and more for every single person on this earth. There has never been and there will never be any shortage for anyone in this world- that is the law of the universe.

On the contrary, if one has more, he will have the capability to help more people and give more to people who are in need. Hence, the need for everybody to strive for abundance and always look for opportunities and ways in which they can get richer and help others. Your getting prosperous doesn't have to hurt others. It should be in such a way that it benefits a lot more.

For the world to treat you well, you need to treat yourself well first. How can you feel like a mover and shaker when you have holes in your underwear. One can say, it's ok that there are holes in my underwear, at least no one is seeing it. But there is a catch here. You know that there are holes in your underwear, and that is enough. Though the world may not be able to see them, you know it and your body can feel it.

Your self-image is determined by how you feel, and feelings are always an inside thing. You are the only one who can make you feel good or bad. It is not your neighbor, your boss, your wife, or your kids. Feeling good about oneself is always an inside job. So hold your head high and always feel good about yourself. Whatever the circumstances may be!

Hence, there is a need to feel good about yourself first and then feeling good about the world. Everything affects everything. Spoil yourself. Be in the best of mood always. Promise yourself that come what may, you will not disappoint yourself. Live your highest self. You deserve this. Life is meant to be a magnum opus.

Even if you are not prosperous as we speak, think prosperity. Always think abundance. Never think of scarcity. As you thinketh, so shall be done to you. Enjoy what you have and then wish for more. Not just wishful thinking, work for more.

Change your belief that you can change your circumstances by working hard and keeping a positive attitude towards everything in life.

"Pamper yourself, nourish your body, keep a clean home, and you will feel blessed by life. The way you walk affects the way you talk. The way you dress affects the way you feel. The care you give to others, you will give to yourself." You may think what is spoiling oneself got to do with prosperity in life? Everything !

The more you feel prosperous, the more you attract prosperity in your life. You cannot say that I will quit living like a miser once I become rich. You have to feel rich to get rich. Prosperity is not necessarily a money thing. It is a lifestyle thing.

LIFE IS SUPPOSED TO BE FUN

As long as you continue to believe something in your life as a disaster, it will unfold as a continuing disaster. Let's say you get fired at fifty and decide your best years are over. As long as you continue to believe that, it will be like that.

Suppose you are recently divorced and you think your life is in shatters and will never be good again. While this may be a life-changing event, and it is okay to be in self-pity for some time, the sooner you get out of this feeling and look at life in a positive way, the better is for you. As long as you see only disaster, you will continue to attract disaster.

Lovers will let you down, bosses will hassle you, accidents will find you, landlords will evict you and it will be a downward spiral; till you decide to take control of your life and change your feeling about events that have happened.

The moment you decide to change that and resolve to look at it as something that happened in the past, and work towards a better future, you will arrive at a better destination a few years or months from then. Events will unfold according to your expectations. The minute you change your beliefs about the situation, your different thoughts will attract different people and new opportunities.

Every disaster in your life is not so much a disaster, as a situation waiting for you to change your mind about it. You say it applies to my illness, my bills, and my drunken husband; you bet it does!

Life is supposed to be fun. Birds wake up singing every day. Babies laugh for no reason at all.

Watch nature in its full glory. It gives one the greatest joy about this thing called life. It's a playful universe.

If you grew up believing that life is meant to be all drudgery and no fun, understand what that means. It's just a belief which you can change in an instant. You are at the controls. You are the captain of your ship. You are the master of your soul. Life is meant to be fun and all happy. Think and live like you cannot fail.

WHERE THERE IS NO ATTACHMENT-THERE IS NO DETACHMENT

The challenge of life is to appreciate everything but not get attached to it. Desperateness to anything results in disappointment. We need to like and love things and have a desire to be, do and have good things in life, but we should not be desperate for them as desperateness leads to discontentment and that leads to unhappiness.

Desperation pulls you into a descending spiral- and the more you worry, the less you get. You have got to sing like you don't need the money, love like you will never get hurt and dance like nobody's watching. It has got to come from your heart if you want it to work.

Desperateness about anything creates an energy around you that pushes that thing away from you, that is the law and that is how it works- always.

Whenever you show desperation at anything, a promotion, someone to call, your husband to quit smoking, or for your boss to show you some appreciation, you push that thing away from you and it takes longer than the time you anticipate, and in some cases do not happen at all. This is because of the unforeseen energy you have created which is keeping you away from them.

However, please note that detachment is not disinterest. It is possible to be detached and still be very much interested. A person who has a keen interest in achieving anything or getting anything knows that it requires effort and hard work and patience. He knows very well that if he does not succeed the first time, there is always a second and then a third chance. He will never lose interest in his task, but he will not be desperate for it and be disheartened or disappointed if he does not get it the first time.

Disinterested people say "Who cares and why bother." Desperate people say "I will die if I don't get this." Determined and interested people say "One way or another, I will get this, and I don't care how long this takes, for I am determined in it and am confident about getting it.

The only way to avoid being desperate is to stop wishing and moaning about how and when things will happen and believing that it will happen, sooner or later. Never get into the trap of "I need X to be happy." The moment you get into this state of mind, you will not be happy as you have tied your happiness to an external factor, which may not be under your control and hence there is an equal chance of it being an unachievable objective. Rather, you do everything to make it work and then you tell yourself, "I don't need this to be happy." Forget it and move on, and more often than not, the results will come.

On a mental and physical level, we are dealing with natural laws. Nature does not understand desperation. Nature seeks balance and you can be both desperate and balanced. Life does not have to be an endless struggle. Let things flow. You can say "I don't understand how this all works." You don't need to understand. You don't understand gravity either. Our challenge is to work with principles- we don't have to understand them.

LIVE TO GIVE

Another principle in working with all human laws is that giving is receiving. If you want something, give it away. However crazy this idea may seem, it is the law of nature. To get a better crop or more seeds, you need to give away the seeds that you have. Want a smile; smile at the person first, want affection, give affection first; want help, help the other person first. This is the law of nature.

For you to get anything in life, first you have to give. You need to connect before you pull. If you follow this law of nature, you will always have abundance in your life. Abundance of money, relationships, happiness, and success. Prosperity is a flow- it's a process of giving and receiving. It cannot be just receiving- ever. The trick to giving is to give without wanting anything back. The moment you attach an expectation to it, of receiving something back in return, either less or nothing happens. The true art of giving is to give without expecting anything in return. There is nothing wrong with wanting to have material possessions in life. Everybody wishes for them, and it is completely okay to wish for the same. And life is meant to grow and achieve more. The only thing to be careful about is while one should wish and enjoy material possession, just make sure you own them and they don't own you.

When we talk of loving another human being, it is giving them the freedom to be who they chose to be and where they chose to be. Love is allowing people to be in your life out of choice. This is again, unattachment. To have something or someone- let go. Getting angry or fighting does not work. You overcome what you don't like by accepting what is – not resisting- and replacing it with something positive. To let go is the mantra. To be detached and let go. If you really love something or somebody, let it be free. If it comes back to you, it is yours. If it does not come back, it was never yours to begin with. This is the principle of all human relationships.

LAW OF EXPANSION

Imagine you are on your way to your favorite destination, up in the sky some twenty thousand feet above the earth and then you hear an announcement that there is a huge turbulence ahead, which has the potential to turn dangerous, so you are advised to buckle up your seat and sit tight.

Would you like your cabin crew to tell you to "Stay calm, and although this will be a bumpy ride, all will be ok and reach destination safe" OR your will like your captain to come up and say, "We will all be killed, we will all be killed and hence start praying." Which of these situations you would like to be in?

Drawing a parallel, think about your everyday life in which you are the pilot of your life. Which approach you would like to have, "we will all be killed" or "stay calm and everything will be alright." This is the essence of positive thinking. There is no guarantee in life, but if you are positive about things and events, there is a greater chance of leading your life in peace and calm.

A negative person sees what is impossible in all situations, however trivial it may be, and he continues to get such situations in life, and a positive person sees the possibilities of life and concentrate and focus on the best outcomes, and they get to keep the good part of life and make things happen.

THE CONSCIOUS AND THE SUBCONSCIOUS

The human brain is made up of two major parts, the conscious brain and the subconscious brain. The conscious brain is responsible for your daily actions and it contains your passing thoughts. Your conscious mind is what dictates what you think and do on a daily basis as you face different situations in life.

In your subconscious mind are the various programs that you were born with and what got recorded as you grew up. Your subconscious mind is responsible for your bodily functions like breathing, digestion, and programs you have created over time as you grew, right from your childhood till date. Subconscious programs are developed over time with repetition of the same act over and over again, which started as a conscious thought but developed into a subconscious thought.

Think about when you took your first driving class. You were new and did not know what to do with what is inside a car, and your trainer teaches you what do to with the clutch, brake, accelerator, horn, indicators, etc. The first time you were told about the same, it triggers a new pathway inside the brain between two neurons. Every time this instruction was repeated and you did the same, this new pathway gets reinforced and it forms a thick band-like strand, and with repetition your act becomes automatic.

Every habit that you have developed in your life happens the same way. The first time you do an act or think a thought or say to yourself something about yourself (good or bad, possible or impossible), you form a new neural connection in the brain.

It is like a small wire that has been connected. With each repetition of the thought or action, another connection gets overlapped in the same neuron, another small wire-like strand, and with each repetition, this keeps on getting added till it becomes a thick neural pathway, like a thick wire, and once that has formed, this action or thought for you becomes automatic and effortless. You will be able to do this next time without any effort as if you are a master at it.

Considering the example of driving as detailed above, every time you repeated the act of changing gears, pressing accelerator or brake, you have formed a neural connection in your subconscious mind and now this act comes automatically for you. Once you learn driving completely with practice, changing gears, applying accelerator to speed up, applying brakes when required becomes effortless for you and you do it subconsciously. Next time you encounter danger in front of your car, your leg will automatically go to the brake pedal and bring the car to a halt. This is how our subconscious and conscious minds work. ANY CONSCIOUS THOUGHT REPEATED OVER A PERIOD OF TIME BECOMES A PROGRAM.

Now imagine having a conscious thought "I am broke" and holding on to that thought for months and years. With constant repetition of this thought over the years, it becomes automatic for you, just like the example above, and then you wonder why you are broke in life. People have created their automatic thoughts about being miserable and broke and then when that manifests in their lives, they wonder why their life is so.

A person who always keeps on repeating to himself/herself, I am not good, I am always late for the meeting, I am not good looking, I am not good at anything, I mess up always, I am too fat, I am too skinny, I don't have friends, etc etc is programing his subconscious mind to believe in these thoughts, and then, as they say, thoughts become things, all these prophecies become true and then we end up blaming God.

Negative thoughts repeated over time develop a negative subconscious, and then we fail to see the good in all opportunities and blame everything outside of ourselves.

Here is the good news. Now that we know that all that we do not have so good in our lives, we are responsible for bringing them on to us, with repeated negative conscious thoughts which developed into negative subconscious behavior, we can change them by a change in our attitude. We need to relook at things and see the positive side of the situation before concluding about the same. Your future depends on your conscious thoughts which you use daily, now with deliberation, and how you select your responses. Just like you can develop subconscious behavior to drive a car, you can develop subconscious behavior to be more successful. But it takes disciplined thinking and some time.

REPETITION IS THE KEY

What happens when you attend a motivational seminar and hear a person speak profoundly and powerfully and motivate you to look at things in a very different way, and you are all pumped up, fully decided that from tomorrow your life will be changed. You come out of the seminar, write down your goals; owning a BMW car, living in a ten thousand sqft home, going on vacation to the US….. and then spend the rest of your day in your usual way and old program.

Few months down the line, you will say this is not working and give up on all that you learned during the motivational seminar.   What has happened here?   Being positive for a day is not enough and will not do anything. Strengthening your mind is like strengthening your body.

You join a gym and lift the dumbbell twenty times and rush to the mirror to see if there is a difference, you will be disappointed. However, if you repeat that for one month, every single day, and then check the mirror, you will see a noticeable difference.

The same goes for daily motivation and life-changing processes. Unless you practice positive thinking daily and feed your mind with positive thoughts on a regular and consistent basis, nothing much will change in your life. However, once you develop a habit of the same and watch very carefully over what you think and do on a daily basis, you will see that you have arrived at a new destination in life, over the years.

If you want to check if your thinking process has changed and if it is working for you, check your life. Your prosperity, your happiness, the quality of your relationships, and even your health are a perfect reflection of your most common conscious thoughts.

THOUGHTS REAP RESULTS

If there is something in your life that you don't like, stop worrying about it, thinking about it, and talking about it. It is a universal truth that if you don't want something in your life, stop it right on its track and do not spend even a minute thinking about it or speaking about it. The energy you put into it by speaking about it keeps it alive. Withdraw your energy and it goes away.

If you refuse to participate in an argument with your husband, even if he comes looking for it, your nonparticipation will dissipate the whole issue and he will also calm down. What happened here is that you did not give this thought energy and it went away. He cannot argue by himself alone.

When you truly let go of something emotionally, it evaporates. It's the law, and it happens every single time.

For more clarity, let's say you are the subject of office gossip. If you start issuing public statements and declaring your innocence, you are adding more fuel to the fire. Ignore it and it will pass. It is not that you are not defending yourself, what I mean to say is that the more you protest, agonize, and jump up and down, you keep the issue alive. Just drop it and it will die a natural death. To sum it up, if you turn your life into a campaign against things, the things you fight will expand. Ignore and it will go away.

WE CHOSE OUR RELATIONSHIPS

John and Mary go on their first dinner date. Mary drops soup on her dress, John says "Here, let me wipe that for you."

Few years down the lane, now husband and wife, John and Mary go out for dinner. Mary spills soup on her dress. John retorts "you are so clumsy."

Same people, same circumstances; different attitude. We chose how we see people. When we want to like someone, we can be so tolerant. When we want to be irritated by people, we see their faults and our reactions match our thoughts.

It is not other people's behavior that determines our feeling towards them- it is our attitude. We need to constantly ask ourselves if we are thinking positive or negative and course-correct as required.

Our brain is like a large fertile land and our thoughts are the seeds that we plant in them. What happens if we don't do anything on the land and leave it untended, weeds will grow automatically. We need to take care of our land, plough it on time, remove the weeds, plant good seeds and take care to protect the seeds from birds, sun, wind. After we do all this for a long period of time, we get to reap the harvest.

In a similar manner, negative is automatic for the brain. We need to stand guard at the gates of our mind and ensure that we always have positive thoughts and not let negative thoughts take control of our mind. If any negative thoughts come, just like the birds coming to pick the seed or sun to dry it, we need to take action to protect our mind and fill it with positive thoughts. The more we practice this on a regular basis, the better will be our overall outlook on life and the better we get out of life.

People who concentrate more on negatives usually defend themselves by saying "I am being realistic." The fact is that you create your reality. You chose how you see the world and the world responds in the same coin.

ATTITUDE OF GRATTITUDE

All spiritual teachings encourage us to give thanks in everything. The law is that the more we express gratitude for what we have, the more abundance comes our way. Always have a sense of gratitude and an inner knowing that life will bless you. If you do this much, you will live a much more abundant and peaceful, and loving life.

FOLLOW YOUR HEART

Your mission in life is not to be without problems; your mission is to be equipped to handle all problems well, and move ahead.

If you choose your attitude, you can love any job you are doing.

If you love what you are doing, you will be happier, do much better and prosper more.

It's a human irony that always the other persons' job seems to be an easy one when compared to you. This feeling cascades up and the person below always feels that the person above him has so little to do, and he has got all the burden of work. We always loathe the person above us and feel his work is so easy and doable while ours is so tough and always with a lot of challenges.

There are no perfect jobs in the world. People pay you to do the work which they either cannot do or don't want to do. All work is to solve a problem or to

make something easy for somebody. If there were no problems to be solved, there would be no job for anybody.

If you don't like your work, there are two options. Change your attitude or change your job.

We are driven by challenges and when life gets too easy, it gets boring. It applies to everything.

It is the challenges that keep us going and excited. No challenge means no excitement.

If your work is too easy, you will get bored too soon. You will lose the drive to do the work and soon work will become a drudgery. It also prevents any growth possibility as you are not learning anything new. Pray for challenges at work, and in general in life. It is the challenges that make us grow. Embrace the challenge and go for it. All your growth lies there.

Another thing to keep in mind always is that you are not working for anybody else - ever. You are not working for your boss, your supervisor, or the owner of your company. You are working for yourself. The day you realize this, you will find work more interesting.

GIVE IT YOUR BEST SHOT-ALWAYS

We are made for excellence and hence it should be natural for us to do the best, every single time. Anything less than excellence should be boring.

There are two reasons why you should always strive for doing the best.

FIRSTLY: You feel happy and satisfied when you give it your best shot. Remember how you felt when you were in school and went to school completing your homework and eager to show it to your teacher. Those feelings grow with you and come up when you are given a project and you complete the project successfully within the deadline, and you head to the meeting room full of confidence and with that high feeling of having accomplished your goal.

SECONDLY: Universe has a way of punishing laziness and arrogance. Enough things will go wrong in your life and you will yourself be not happy with a half-hearted effort. Casual effort gives casual results. It takes more than talent to stay at the top.

When you enjoy your work, you get up every day excited and look forward to the day with great enthusiasm. The desire to do something better every day keeps you going. And people who do better each day, know that it requires a lot of practice to do good and be the best in any field. Repetition is the key. The best of the best in any field practice every day without a miss and give their best. Anthony Robbins, one of the best motivational speakers of this current age, was once asked just before his mega seminar "Tony, you would have given this talk a hundred times over your lifetime. How long did you prepare for today's seminar?" Without thinking even a bit he said "Three Hours." Despite his huge success, Anthony takes no shortcuts, no chances. He is committed to delivering excellence in his work, every single time. That is why the statement "It takes more than talent to stay at the top."

Always do more than you are paid for and one day you will be paid more than you work. When you give fifty percent of your effort, you suffer much more than your boss. He may lose a few dollars because of your low efficiency, but you lose your enthusiasm and your self-esteem, and a whole chunk of your life. Enjoying what you do is a choice. You give your best not because you have to impress people. You give your best because that is the only way to enjoy your work.

There are no medals for spending a lifetime doing something you hate. Your life will only work when you take full responsibility for your work. If you know in your heart that you are in the wrong kind of work, change your job and do something you love.

CHOSE YOUR CAREER WISELY

It is possible to do what you love and get paid for it. It will require discipline, time, and hard work. That does not mean quit your job and start working on what you love. You need to plan properly. You need to keep at what you are working on currently and do what you love and what is your passion during your free time. Start small and keep on increasing your time on your passion and build it up slowly till it gives you enough to replace your regular work and income. Once you have built it to that level, you can switch and do what you love full-time. Life becomes a song then and you will not need any external motivation to do what you are doing. You will be happier and do much better, now that you are doing what you love and like. Your energy level will be different and your commitment will be different.

Stop playing the martyr, never putting time aside just for ourselves. If you cannot do things that you love in your leisure time, it's doubtful you will ever allow yourself to work in a job you really love.

STILL SEARCHING FOR YOUR PASSION

It is a fact that for the majority of us, we end up in life where we had little choice and where we had little say when it came to selecting our profession. For a lot of many of us, we ended up enrolling in a course which was selected by our parents or our well-wishers, either because they were the decision-makers for our lives or because we were completely lost as to what is to be done with our lives.

We chose our vocation based on somebody else's judgment as to what they thought is good for us and will allow us to excel. You took up appropriate hobbies and did what was "expected."

While we are doing the best we can at the current moment, we are not happy at the same and feel work is a burden, and if for the paycheck which helps us pay bills, we would have quit today.

How do we find our passion and how to make our passion our profession is the biggest question for all of us? Simplify your life, quit doing things out of habit, switch off the TV for a month and notice what

excites you. Try new things and discover what feelings you have while you do this new thing.

Does it make it easy for you to get out of bed early, and you do not want to take rest while doing this;

do you forget time and even forget yourself while doing this and you can put in as much effort as required; this is where your passion lies. Do this for the rest of your life and you will never be short of ideas and energy to do this, and this can be your profession benefitting you monetarily too.

To find what you seek, you may need to try different things before you find what you really like doing and is passionate about. To find, you have to seek.

If you have lost your life's direction, you cannot find that by some casual talk with friends or wasting away time in front of the TV. Give yourself a break and some quiet time and space to examine what counts for you. Most importantly, get comfortable with the idea of doing what you like. To do what you love doing, you have to first believe that it is possible.

Many people don't know what they want- and they are upset because they are not getting it. If you don't know exactly what you want, figure out what is closest to it and take some spare time doing it, and go from there.

HARD WORK BEATS TALENT WHEN TALENT DOES NOT WORK HARD

Leading a team is a talent. Caring for people is talent. Making people feel welcome is a talent. Teaching is a talent. Parenting is a talent. Being the best in whatever you do is making use of your talent. Too often we underestimate our talents and try to be good at other things. We try to imitate people and do things that others do, and then when the results are not that great, we conclude we don't have talent.

A potter should concentrate on making good pottery; when he tries to be a singer is when he finds that he is not so good at it and then becomes disappointed. Don't measure your abilities with others. We each have unique talents and abilities and when we compare that with others we are disappointed. Do what you can do and do it to the best of your ability. Fulfillment comes from developing our gifts and not wishing for someone else's.

Talent is useful but it isn't everything. Hard work when coupled with talent can do miracles. Without hard work, talent is not of much use. It is our attitude and hard work that will make our talent stand apart.

Attitude + Hard Work = Genius

Onlookers and underachievers put a lot of emphasis on talent. For them, talent, or lack of it, is a great excuse to do nothing. If there is an outstanding quality common among all great people of the world, meaning people who have achieved something of significance in life, it is not talent, but focus and hard work. Doing it again and again. Repetition is the key.

Many people turn their hobbies into their full-time work, and the transition from hobby to livelihood is very gradual. It is possible to make a living doing something you love. The world is a market place and once you develop a skill that solves people's problems, they will pay you. Of note: people who convert their past times into their profession don't spend much time watching them. Living other people's lives is no match for your living your own. If you want to earn a living doing what you love, your hobby is a possible source of income; in case you have multiple hobbies, think about it and see which one gives you the most kick and keeps you engaged and motivated to do more and more; chose that and get to work on that. Your hobby is a possible source of income and if you don't have leisure activities, your options are limited.

COURSE CORRECT AND WALK A NEW PATH

My father always did what he wanted to do. He was a chemical engineer and was responsible for the complete installation and commissioning of many solvent extraction plants across the country. At other times, he was a kalarippayattu fighter (a form of martial arts practiced in the southern part of India), a judo master, an excellent cook, a great teacher, and a great philosopher.

I grew up believing that work was whatever you wanted to do. I quit studying law and entered into IT and then moved to ITES, a start-up venture of my own with the collaboration of few friends, and then into training and coaching, and finally into Entrepreneurship.

I now spend most of my time working with organizations and individuals on developoing

Leadership skills and Emotional intelligence techniques to have better control of life, both personal and professional. This was something I cherished from my childhood days- to make a difference in people's lives and to teach them how to live better and happier.

The purpose of writing this book is to let people know that you should course correct when you realize that you are not moving in the right direction and find what you love, and go after it. To find meaning and excitement in your work and to lead a fulfilling life, you need to follow your calling in life. And once you find it, you should have the courage and willingness to take it to completion. What saddens me is that so many people get the work they hate, often with rather lame excuses. What I notice is that we chose careers that fit our belief system.

Let's say you wanted to play cricket but you became an engineer to please your dad. Dad's words are ringing in your ears "You have had opportunities I never had." While most of us succumb to Dad's pressure, there are few who will find a way to convince his parents around. What you have to understand is that you can't live your life through someone else.

While you are sacrificing yourself to please your parents, you are postponing your growth. You are not here to fulfill the dreams of your parents- find your dream and work on fulfilling that. Why do you want to spend your life doing something you don't like? Do what you love and you will find work interesting and meaningful.

You say "Should I quit my IT job and pursue my passion?" There is something called a calculated risk. Do not quit your job till you have mastered yourself and developed the necessary skills needed to convert your passion to a profession. Do something each day to improve on what you like and a day will reach when your income from what you love doing will either be equal to or surpass your current income. Quit then, and continue doing what you love throughout your life. Develop your abilities, expand your knowledge, study, and create a demand for your skill- and then move to what you love forever. You will not only earn better, but you will also sleep better.

DO WHAT YOU LOVE

Many men go fishing all their lives without knowing that it is not the fish they are after-Henry David Thoreau.

If you are working just for money, the chance is great that you won't be happy and you probably won't make much money. It's the universe's way of prodding you to do something you really love. When you love what you do, you are less attached to money, and you usually make more of it.

Money is a game- you win by playing the game and not agonizing over the score. You may appreciate money, but dedication goes way beyond money. Whatever work you are doing currently, you are competing against people who love what they do and if you don't love what you do, you will be blown away by competition, because there is a huge difference between one who loves his craft and one who does it to pay his bills.

There is always room for excellence. And being excellent at your craft is again a matter of attitude. Change your attitude about what you are doing, and your work will get more interesting and doable.

Sometimes change can happen out of quite desperation. When you reach a stage where you realize "enough is enough" and you are sick and tired of being broke, you will change, and change for the better. But why wait to reach that stage, when you can make the change with a little thought and also making your passion your profession, starting small at first and then building it to that level where it becomes your primary source of income and livelihood.

Doing what you love will very often make you more prosperous in the long run. And sometimes you realize that doing what you love does not require that much of money, to be peaceful and enjoy what you are doing.

For example, if you are a high profile CEO of a company with all the benefits of a high salary package, huge bungalow, nice car, and all the benefits of being in that post and then you realize that your real love is breeding horses and teaching horse riding, you will realize, when you become a riding instructor, that you don't need the penthouse and the nice cars to pursue your passion. We oftentimes buy toys to take our minds off the fact that we hate our job. And then we fall into the debt trap where we have to keep the job to clear the loans.

Whatever you do for a living is a vehicle to connect with people. Whether or not you are fulfilled depends on how you serve other people.

SERVICE BEFORE SELF

When serving other people becomes your primary motive to do work, you will automatically find your connect and you will feel more interested in doing the work. Serving is knowing that there is joy in giving a part of yourself that is unique to you. It's not about your job description. It's your philosophy of life. Whatever profession you are in life, as long as your motive is to serve others, you are on the right track and you will find fulfillment in your work. It's not about you. It's about others.

As Zig Zigler, the great motivator and author says "You can get anything in life as long as you help the other person get what he wants." This is the essence of human life. To help others get what they want. And you will automatically see that things are turning in your favor and you start getting all that you want. Putting others first is the basic principle of all human endeavors.

If you are a teacher and you tell yourself "What do I matter? The kids don't care about algebra." If you are teaching sixth grade, your mission is not algebra, your mission is children. If you are a banker, your mission is not balance sheets, it is people. Joy comes from combining effort and imagination. It comes from choosing to be involved and saying " I can help." It is not what you do, it's how you do.

Whatever profession you are in life, you can do what everyone else does or you can use your imagination and do something else. In whatever you do, make service your primary motto. The moment you shift your focus from yourself to others, the whole game changes. Let the spotlight be on others. When you give away the need to be important and the need to feel that others should acknowledge you, you are on the right track and all work will become a song.

According to the Law of Dharma (Sanskrit word for your purpose), we each have unique talents which we are here to discover. When we express those talents, we find joy. As per the law of the universe, when we ask ourselves what can we give instead of what can we get, we discover our talents and purpose.

When you are in the flow, you will realize that money is a byproduct and that your purpose in life is what makes you more excited. Be on the lookout and everything will fall into place. Once you find your purpose, go after it.

FINDING YOUR PURPOSE

Our purpose in life is not to be worried about what will happen to other works if all start doing what their passion is or what they love. We need to understand that all of us are moving in different directions and life has a strange way of bringing order in life. We are all in different spaces and when you move to do what your calling in life is, there will be someone who will move to fill in your shoes. Different people like to do different things. The calling of each one in life is different.

It is not that when we start doing what we love in life, our problems will disappear or that we will have lesser problems.

Our purpose in life is not to have lesser problems, our purpose is to be excited about what we are doing and to understand that our best shot at prosperity is by doing what we love. Love is energy. Everything you do with love is infused with energy and when you do something with energy, it is bound to bring you more happiness and prosperity.

Doing what you love is not a recipe for a problem-free life or a life with lesser problems- it is just that it helps you cope with all problems and issues in a happier way. Being happy in whatever you do is the essence.

BEING HAPPY-NO MATTER WHAT

Being happy is a project, whatever you care to name. You start wherever you are with whatever you have and do everything in your hands to make it a success. It's more about effort than luck. And the key to the success of this project is in your hands.   You own it completely, and your enthusiasm will determine what you make out of it.

When you care about something enough, you will have all the energy and the enthusiasm to do it with all your heart, and work will not be a burden for you. No one else has to motivate you when you are passionate about your work and you are on a mission. Challenges are inevitable. You will have setbacks. You will encounter people, close to you, who will either criticize you or discourage you from doing what you are doing.

You will have your own family members who will have their own opinions on why what you are doing is not the right thing and why you will fail. It is during these testing times that your enthusiasm and your belief in yourself are the only factors that will carry you through all such negative people.

You will go through frustrations, but in your heart you know you are on course. Sure you need plenty of determination, but your passion is your foundation.

Vitality comes from a sense of purpose and you owe it to yourself and other people to do what excites you. There should be that fire in you to do something with your life. Vitality comes with a sense of purpose.

The world is full of people who do work halfheartedly and is lukewarm in approach and who get burned out without ever having been on fire. Following your dream is no guarantee of an easy life.

Life will become more challenging, and therein lies your chance to discover what stuff you really are made up of. It gives you a chance to rise above your limiting beliefs and blossom- to see what you are capable of.

And please remember, wherever you are- you are not stuck- you are a human being and not a tree. Make new resolutions, have a solid game plan, and go for it. The sky is not the limit for you. You can even go beyond the clouds.

YOU CAN EITHER MAKE EXCUSES- OR YOU CAN HAVE IT ALL- YOU CANNOT HAVE BOTH

Our life unfolds before us as per our deepest thoughts and our beliefs. If you have unfulfilled dreams, analyze your excuses. We are not honest when it comes to ourselves. As they say "if your why is very clear and strong enough, you can withstand any how and what." We excuse ourselves by saying things are impossible when things are inconvenient.

We like to be in our comfort zone and avoid what is uncomfortable for us and that which requires us to step out. We convince ourselves that we have no choice when the fact is that we never tried. Starting off to do a new thing which is close to your heart may be tough, it may require that you spend some more time on that, it may require you to learn a new skill, it may require you to work double of what you are doing currently, it may require long hours at work, but it is all worth in the end.

You will come out of the other end happy and prosperous, with a feeling of great accomplishment and you will be pleased with yourself. Impossible is just an excuse for people who don't want to take any responsibility.

IMPOSSIBLE ALSO SAYS "I AM POSSIBLE"

Take the case of Roger Bannister who broke the 4-minute mile record on May 06, 1954. Before this date, it was considered an impossible task for the human body to run a mile under 4 minutes. So many athletes had tried achieving this feat and had tried all possible methods to complete this run, but none had achieved.

Scientists and physiologists during that time had done a lot of study about the human body and confirmed that it is impossible for the human body to run a mile under 4 minutes. They had said that if anybody tries to run a mile under 4 minutes, his heart will explode due to the pressure exerted by the blood vessels and such a person will die. Everybody till his time, believed it to be true.

Roger Bannister, an English middle-distance athlete, and a neurologist chose not to believe in this and decided to attempt running a mile under 4 minutes. On May 06, 1954, Roger Bannister ran a mile under 4 minutes at Oxford and proved everybody wrong. What is interesting is that his record lasted just 46 days. Once Roger was able to cross this, people started believing this was possible and within that year many other athletes were able to run a mile under 4 minutes.

This goes on to prove that all limitations are in our minds, and if a man decides, he can achieve anything.

Nick Vujicic is an Australian American Christian evangelist who was born with tetra-amelia syndrome, a rare disorder, characterized by the absence of arms and legs. Born in 1982, Nick was initially ridiculed and made a target of school bullies, and he fell into severe depression. Although he was an otherwise healthy baby, he had no arms and legs. At the age of 8, he contemplated suicide, and at the age of 10 he tried to drown himself in a bathtub, but his love for his parents prevented him from following through.

"As long as I try, there's always a chance of getting up. Its not the end until you give up."

Nick prayed very hard that God would give him arms and legs, and initially told God, that if his prayers remained unanswered, Nick would not praise him indefinitely. However, a key turning point in his faith came when his mother showed him a newspaper article about a man dealing with severe disability. Vujicic realized he wasn't unique in his struggles and began to embrace his lack of limbs. After this Nick realized his accomplishments could inspire others and became grateful for his life.

Nick gradually figured out how to live a full life, without limbs, adapting many of the daily skills limbed people accomplished without thinking. Nick writes with two toes on his left foot and a special grip that slid into his big toe. He knows how to use a computer and can type up to 45 words per minute using the "heel and toe" method. He has learned to throw tennis balls, play drum pedals, get a glass of water, comb his hair, brush his teeth, answer the phone and shave, in addition to participating in golf, swimming, and even sky diving.

During secondary school, he was elected captain of MacGregor state in Queensland and worked with the student council on fundraising events for local charities and disability campaigns. When he was seventeen, he started to give talks at his prayer groups, and later found his nonprofit organization, Life Without Limbs. Nick travels the world giving hope to people to never give up, however challenging the circumstances are. His favorite quote is "I love my life because I have found my purpose."

"Along the way, you might fall down...sometimes in life, you might fall down and can't find the strength to get back up....do you think you have hope? Because I tell you, I am down here and I have no arms and no legs...it would be impossible for me to get up, but it's not. "

All disabilities and shortcomings are in our minds, and the moment we challenge them and rise above our limitations, we can achieve anything in life. We need to not give up until we have given it our all.

Take a look at your limitations. When odds are stacked against you, you develop the mental toughness, and the strength you derive becomes your secret weapon. Pressure is good. Coal becomes diamond under pressure. If there was no pressure, there would be no diamond. Just like that, humans need to be put under pressure sometimes to grow and shine.

There is a pattern amongst people who achieve their dreams- they start from a long way behind. Roger Bannister had the entire world hypothesis against him that it is impossible for the human body to propel itself so fast as to cover a mile under 4 minutes. Nick was born with no arms and legs. However, it was their mental and physical challenges that propelled them to achieve what they have done.

We always have a choice to do or not to do; to be or not to be. To rise above our challenges or be mediocre. If you are not doing anything, it's because your focus is somewhere else and you have directed your energies elsewhere.

The question is not "Why this is impossible?" The question is "What am I unwilling to do?" When you owe up your accountability and have a "never say die attitude" and a "come what may" attitude, life then starts to support you. As they say, when you change the way you look at things, the things you look at will change. Even Gods move for the person who is ready to help himself and willing to go that extra mile.

As it has been said in the Bible: You move one step towards God and he will move two steps towards you.

PERMISSION TO SUCCEED

Jump in and then find your way out. You get excited about things only after you start. You take the plunge and then you feel excited and energetic. And your excitement and energy will drive you to achieve whatever you set out to.

We often make the mistake of saying "When we get the energy, we will begin." You need to start first to feel the energy. Don't wait to feel the surge of energy and then start working. This is reverse flow. You get the energy and the enthusiasm after you begin. It's your involvement that triggers the energy. The secret is to make a start wherever you are with whatever you have and go from there.

You will never be hundred per cent ready for anything in life. Neither will you be absolutely sure about being successful. You take your chances and move ahead. Have faith in yourself, believe in your work, and confidence that you will achieve what you have set to achieve, and nothing can stop you.

About starting things, are you ever ready before you make a speech? How much so ever you prepare, you still feel butterflies in your stomach just before the delivery.

Marriage? Are you ever ready and confident that everything is going to be perfectly alright once you get married? Are you prepared for what follows? Not likely. You prepare as best you can and then take the plunge.

Nothing in life is predictable a hundred per cent. There is no guarantee that you won't fail. You prepare as best as you can, and then you start without knowing all the answers and without any guarantee.

To sum up: You get motivated by doing things, and not thinking about them. It is action and action alone that gets you excited and gives you the energy to do things. Action reveals you opportunities.

When you decide to do something and you really want to do it, do not agonize over it for days or months. Do not spend much time planning and thinking when to start.

Start immediately and take daily steps which will take you closer to your desired objective. Don't get into too much analysis or you will get into paralysis of analysis and never be able to start or take off. And if you are not able to start and do something daily, you will get stuck and all projects will be either incomplete or never would start.

So many people chicken out at the slightest encounter of challenges and find reasons for not finishing it and tie it to all external sources. They never take time to look inside of themselves and realize what went wrong and how it can be corrected. They are too busy putting the blame on external factors, rather than work on their own shortcomings, and see what could have been better and yielded different results which would have helped them reach their goal.

Only commit to something which you know you will follow through. Under promise and over delivery is an apt statement. Always strive to do more, and give more, in whatever endeavor you are in. Keep up your commitment and do whatever you say you will do. Live by your word. Only when you live up to the commitment that you have given yourself that you will believe in yourself.

GET UNCOMFORTABLE

Addiction to comfort is the root cause of all failures in human endeavor. The ships that feel safe at the harbors never go anywhere and achieve nothing. You need to set your sails and go out into the rough ocean. Only when you weather the rough ocean and face the challenges that you will be able to catch a bounty.

Some ships never sail out of the harbor for the fear of the unknown and the comforts of the harbor. Don't be like that ship. Roar out, meet challenges, face tough situations, improvise yourself, learn new things, and only then will you be able to achieve your dream and live the life you always wanted. A smooth sea never made a good sailor.

Make fewer rules for life- life ought to be like this, it ought to be like that, and the list goes on ....take life as it comes and prepare yourself for a new day every day. Take kaizen steps and make sure you are inching towards your goal every day. Every day that passes should bring you one step closer to your goal.

And to do all this, you need courage. Courage is better rewarded than IQ. In life, too often people with lesser IQ outperform people with higher IQ; they get better jobs, make more money, and are happier in life. Rewards come when we risk our reputation or our money or both.

Get scared over something significant. Don't play small and timid. There is value to having people in our life who will challenge us- it's just that they will be less comfortable. But it is these people who will make us push our boundaries and make us do something significant. The world is a tough place and nature's laws are ruthless. You either follow the laws and get ahead or ignore them and fall behind.

Look out for the scorpions in your life. They don't mind drowning if they drag you down. Following your dreams does not mean you are soft. The world is a tough place and the weaker you are, the more foxes will get you- as an easy target.

One day a frog was sitting by a stream. A scorpion came and said "Mr. Frog, I would like to cross the stream, but I am a scorpion and cannot swim. Would you be so kind as to swim across with me on your back?" And the frog said: "But you are a scorpion and scorpions sting frogs." Said the scorpion "Why would I sting you? I want to get to the other side. "Ok," said the frog, "Climb on my back and I will take you"

They were just halfway across the stream when the scorpion stung the frog. Writhing in agony, and with his last breath, the frog said "Why did you do that? Now we will both drown." "Because," said the scorpion, " I am a scorpion and scorpions sting frogs."

Look out for the scorpions. There will be people around you who would want to drag you down and they don't mind drowning in the process. And most of the time, you will find them as a relative or a close friend. Sometimes you have to stand and fight. Do what is right as per your calling and your gut feeling. Do what is fair. Do what is good for all. And ask yourself "Do I feel this is the right thing to do" If your answer is a yes, go ahead and do it.

Take your position, irrespective of whether other people are going to like you or think you are nice. Sometimes doing the right thing is not easy and not always people may like it. That's a choice you have to make- every single day. You will always have two choices- try to get everyone like you or agree with you OR do what you think is right and not what pleases everybody. You should be guided by your inner conscience.

IF YOU DO WHAT YOU HAVE ALWAYS DONE-YOU WILL GET WHAT YOU HAVE ALWAYS GOT

They say the definition of insanity is doing the same thing over and over again and expecting different results. It takes courage to chart a new course in life, a new career, a completely new chapter, and go in the direction of your dreams. Ask any person who has achieved their dreams, as to what prompted them to change course and walk a new path and how they succeeded, you will get only one answer, they asked themselves the question "IF THE WORST HAPPENED, COULD I DEAL WITH IT." When the answer is Yes, they take the plunge. Taking a new course may be quite challenging, and full of doubts, but your belief in yourself will carry you through any challenges that life throws at you.

It is not a negative approach to ask "What's the worst that could happen." It's a way of measuring your commitment. Break your fears into specific possibilities and risk-taking becomes more fun. And the answer to this question will completely depend upon your faith in the whole process and more importantly, your faith in yourself.

LIVE IN THE NOW

Don't wait for tomorrow or the day after or sometime in the future. We all put off living for tomorrow. When I have a good bank balance, when I am in good health, when my kids grow up, are some of the common excuses for putting things off to the future.

Don't overthink, learn to live in the now. There is nothing called yesterday and nothing called tomorrow. It is only the NOW that is there. Everything else is transient or illusionary. It's a NOW, followed by another NOW and then another NOW.

It's a series of NOWs that make up your life. Take your best shot, give it your everything and forget about the score. The less you worry about winning and what other people think, the better you will perform.

FORCING THINGS NEVER WORK

Effortless work is what yields results. See how effortless is nature in all its glory. The flowers bloom without any effort, the sun rises without effort, the air flows effortlessly and that is how nature unfolds before us. The real power comes when you are relaxed. Try doing something when you are angry or in an agitated mood, you will not be able to do anything, and even if you attempt at doing, you will end up faltering. You are more powerful when you are not trying to prove that you are powerful.

Keep Your Cool:

Have you ever noticed getting angry is not the best option always; in fact majority of the time. Getting angry is an emotional state in which thinking brain stops thinking and is in an overwhelmed state where reason has flown out of the window. Maintain your calm in all circumstances, it does not come easy and needs self-awareness and lots of practice. But it is a learnable skill that can be mastered over time.

Opposition Is Good:

Be it in your daily life or politics, opposition is good, as long as it is constructive and reasonable. Don't hate people who do not align with your view of things. Accept differences and focus on the task at hand. Paying too much attention to people who don't agree with you drains your energy and you get off track. Acknowledge them and continue doing what you are doing.

BE AN INVERSE PARANOID

I always believe that the whole universe is conspiring to do me good. When you operate from that mindset, everything that you encounter in your journey will be pleasant.

If you think the world is against you, it perhaps is. Stop operating from that mindset. Blaming other people, the weather, your parents, your neighbor etc never works. Successful people do not look at things outside of themselves as the reason for things that are good or not so good, they always look inside for solutions, and therein lies the true solution. Solutions to all your problems lie inside of you. Look within.

Be Consistent And Persistent: Consistency and persistency against all odds wins the day. Ask any person who has achieved something great in life, and you will get to hear that their unrelenting persistence despite all odds is what helped them through and made them what they are today. When you demand more of yourself than others demand of you, nothing

can stop you from achieving what you have set out to achieve. Casual and half-hearted attempts have never worked and will never work. Determination and consistency of effort is required for any endeavor of significance.

FOCUS ON WHAT YOU WANT AND NOT WHAT YOU DON'T WANT IN LIFE

Our mind is a strange organ. It will constantly think what you tell it not to think. Say I ask you now not to think of a dancing monkey while you are taking a bath today. How muchsoever you try, your mind will constantly think of the dancing monkey and the more you try not to think of it, the more it will. Hence the saying goes, focus on what you want and not what you don't want. Whatever you think about consistently has a strange way of manifesting itself in your life. The more you focus on a thing, the more it will appear before you.

Have you ever noticed if you think of your dream car very often, when you go out on the roads, you will suddenly start seeing more of that car on the roads now? It would be as if suddenly more people have started buying that car. As per the law, whatever you focus more on, manifests. Hence the need to focus more on things you want. If you see yourself falling while skiing, you will invariably fall; if you think of not getting a parking lot for your car today, you will end up not getting the parking that day. By a strange turn of events, whatever you think about, presents before you.

Hence always, as a principle, think of and focus on what you want in life. Just think about, speak about, and talk about things you want. Always. Ask a golfer if they visualize putting the ball or missing the hole. They will always tell you, they visualize and think and talk about completing the stroke and the ball smoothly sliding into the hole. Ask a batsman if he thinks or focuses on missing the ball every time he swings the bat, and he will say he focuses only on hitting the ball beyond the boundary- every single time. The more people focus on things they want, the more they get.

Fear is a killer, not just in sports, in every arena of life. Where there is fear, happiness is not.

When you concentrate on what you fear and create those disaster pictures in your mind, the more you are headed for disaster.

All children should have a chance to play some sport- not for the trophies they get, but for the lessons they learn. It's not where you start. It's how you finish.

Shad Helmstetter in his book " What to say when you talk to yourself" says that you need be very careful about what you think, say, and focus on. He goes on to say, always, as a rule; think, speak and focus on positive things and things you really want in life. The more you get into this practice of thinking positive, talking positive, and focusing on positive things, the better your life will unfold before you and you will see positive changes in your overall wellbeing and life in general. Do not think or say or focus on things you don't want in your life, even if it is currently present in your life. If you are in a not-so-good relationship with your spouse, don't keep on focussing on that. Instead, focus on the good days you have spent together and how happy you were during those times. Think of the things you did in that state and the universe has a strange way of bringing to your life what you focus on. If you are in debt, do not think of the bills and the debts but think of abundance and focus on having more money, and then you will see the tide turn in your favor. The law of the universe will be at play.   When the student is ready, the teacher appears. Once we decide to do a thing, the means appear. And these are no coincidences- if you follow the law- they will be regular.

GOOD OR BAD- RIGHT OR WRONG- ITS YOUR PERSPECTIVE: DON'T FIGHT THE LAW

Once upon a time in a faraway country, there lived a very wealthy and famous king who basked in glamor, glory, and luxury. He had all that he wanted. Sadly, this king never knew or believed in God. He was a man of his own. But this king had a servant, whom he loved far above other servants and so he made him Chief of all his servants. Unlike the king, the servant trusted in God and believed God was good and whatever he does, he does for a good reason. He was a good servant and loved his master and followed him wherever he went.

The king was a man who loved a lot of things, but above all; he loved to *hunt*. Every evening, he and his beloved servant will set out into the woods to hunt for animals. A day came, the king and his servant had gone into the woods to hunt, suddenly a wild bear attacked the king. They fought bravely with the bear and eventually killed it but not before the bear bit off the king's right thumb. The king was so angry about losing a finger that he hated himself so much and was ashamed of himself. He cursed God and blamed him for his lost finger. His beloved servant consoling told him that whatever God does was *good*, and he does so for a *good* reason. The King's anger was kindled so much against his servant that he ordered him to be thrown into prison. The servant was thrown into the prison and the king got himself another servant.

After some days, the king with his new servant set out into the woods to hunt wild animals. Behold, a tribe from afar kingdom surrounded and kidnapped them. The king and his servant were then bound in chains. It was a feast of their gods which demands for the sacrifice of a *"complete man."* The king watched as the men slaughtered and sacrificed his servant to their gods, he wept bitterly. Soon it was his turn to be killed.

On a close inspection, as he was about to be slain, one of the men noticed that the king was missing a finger and he ordered that he be released and set free at once. This he said because the king was incomplete, therefore unfit and abominable to be used as a sacrifice to their gods. With that, the king was set free and he went home.

The king then commanded that his beloved servant be released from the prison and brought before him. The king hugged him tightly and said *"Truly, your God is good, and whatever he does, is for a good reason".* But continued the king, if the Lord is good and everything he does is for a good reason, why did he let me throw you into prison? Do you also believe he has a good reason? the king asked.

Smiling, the servant replied "yes I do, *the Lord already knew you would be kidnapped to be used as a sacrifice, he also knew that the sacrifice would require a complete man, so he saved me by letting you throw me into prison. If not, I would have been the one kidnapped with you in the woods today and sacrificed to their Gods* ". So you see, continued the servant, *the Lord is truly good and everything He does is for a good reason. The king nodded in agreement and hugged his servant.*

We can spend our whole life fighting everything out, this is good, that is bad, god is good, god is bad.....and the list goes on. We label the events as a disaster or a good event, based on our perceptions of things and events. There is nothing called right or wrong, it is how we look at it.

So long as you will keep on thinking that things are going wrong/bad, it will go the same way. Change your perspective.

You miss a flight and you are all upset and kicking. You are angry about your getting up late, angry about the traffic, angry about the ticket counter lady, and about everything that happened that led to your missing your flight. Or you can just take another flight and move ahead. There is no point in applying logic to everything in your life. When you fight life, life wins- always.

You apply for a job and you believe you have all the qualifications and experience required for the job but you end up not getting the job. You start blaming yourself, you are not so good, and indulge in self-pity. However, this does not work. You wonderfully argue your case with a whole lot of logic, but life does not work logically. You miss some, you get some. If you want to have a happy and peaceful life, stop labeling things as good or bad.

A basketball player at the peak of his career slipped between tracks and lost both his limbs. He was wheelchair-bound and his dreams were shattered. He decided not to consider this as a disability and work on it. He restarted his play and became an outstanding wheelchair athlete.

Upon being interviewed, he said, I can't think what I would be like if I had both my legs. I am happy in the space that I am in right now. I know what I have done. I know what I want to do. And that's exciting.

Take another case of a fifty-two-year-old man who regained his eyesight after a major surgery. He had been blind all his life but thanks to the development in science, he was able to regain his sight back. But now when he analyzed his life, he was not happy with what he was. He considered his life spent a waste and his accomplishments as paltry. He gets depressed and dies within a year.

THINK RIGHT

There are only two ways to look at the world:

The world is a mess: Have you ever realized how much it drains you both emotionally and physically to constantly find fault in things around you.   Finding fault in everything, agonizing that the world is not fair, that some people cheat and steal and kill, some people are lazy, some people eat too much, some people are so fat... and the list goes on. It does not serve any purpose to you if you continue to look at the negative side of the world and see it as a mess. However, if we are doing something about it, in changing the situation, helping it become better by serving people, be a change agent, the situation makes a little more sense. However, judging people and situations from a distance and without fully understanding the same serves no purpose. If you want to make a difference and do something about it, it's a different matter. The agonizing does not work. The doers of the world do not agonize-they ACT.

The world is alright as it is: There is perfect harmony in the world and nature. Everything happens as per natural laws and it is flawless. The sun rises in the east and sets in the west every single day for the last six thousand years; flowers bloom as per seasons and the stars shine at night as it has been happening since humanity is known to exist.

We cannot wish away the sickness, the pain, the unrest in the world as they are all part and parcel of growing up. We should aim at contributing to the causes of the world, in whatever little way we can. Giving is happiness. You find perfect joy and happiness when you live with an intention to give something. Nothing feels better than that.

Wishful Thinking:

Our mind is always in a wishful world. If this was like this, if she behaved more politely, if he had picked up the socks, if he had loved me more, if my kids were more disciplined.....and the list goes on. Sometimes we are so dependent on external factors to make us happy that we stop living in the present moment.

We have a "worry hierarchy" and the most important things get worried about first.

One of my close friend had a regular complaint of frequent headaches, and her daily life was very much disturbed because of that. One day she fell while playing badminton and cracked her kneecap. It was major and required hospitalization, surgery, and two months of bed rest. Now, she does not complain of headaches. Her major worry now is the fractured kneecap. This is called the worry hierarchy. This is how life is.

We need to stop finding ways to be worried and irritated all the time. Things will happen and we need to relax or drop some of the rules in our head to find happiness, and we get less irritated when the world does not behave as we expect it to.

Make a conscious decision "No one is going to ruin my day." We make a pact with ourselves that nothing and nobody can mess with my day, not the arrogant bank clerk, no parking attendant, no traffic cop, no waiter, nobody can mess with my 24 hours. In the bigger scheme of things of life, these incidents are very insignificant and need not get so much of our attention that it spoils even a small part of our day.

There are alternatives to getting angry. The lesser rules we have as to how others ought to behave or how things need to unfold in our lives, the happier we will be.

CONTROL YOUR THOUGHTS- CONTROL YOUR LIFE

You cannot control the environment, the weather, the behavior of other people, or their opinion about you. The only thing that you have control over and that's the only thing that matters- is your own thoughts. Externals never make us happy. We need to have an internal locus of control and not be driven by external factors or people.

As long as you are in a habit of finding happiness from external things or people, it will be short-lived and within 24 hours you will be finding things to complain about.

Whether you were abused in traffic, your best friend forgot your birthday, you bumped against the table and your toe is swollen, you lost your earring in the market- all these incidents can make you upset, but realize it was not the incident per se that was disturbing. It was your thoughts about the incident and the way you interpreted it. You may feel anybody in that position will get upset-NO. Most people may. All our lives we are conditioned to think certain thoughts about things, and it is these thoughts that make us happy or unhappy. The good news is that we can change that in an instant. Change your thoughts. You improve your quality of life by working on your thoughts, and your thoughts affect your feeling.

STOP CHASING RESULTS

Have you ever noticed that with almost everything we do in life, we are chasing results. And in the process of chasing results, we are not being mindful of our present and we always are thinking about things happening in the future. We find it very tough to be in the present and most of our time is spent regretting the past or fearing the future.

We need to be mindfully aware of our situations and with practice, we can live in the moment. Refuse to live in a hurry. Our belief system is constantly telling us "There is not enough time." Change it. Remind yourself there is enough time to do the right thing. We seem to be in a hurry always. Hurry to catch the flight, hurry for lunch, hurry for the meeting, hurry to get back home from work- SLOW DOWN. Say to yourself "however long it takes, I will not hurry."

Be more observant. Enjoy what you are doing currently; having a meal, taking your dog for a walk, talking to your friend, listening to a song- everything- just slow down and take it all in. Enjoy, savor and relish the food, hear every note, pay attention to what the other person is saying; just be in the moment. Be fully mindful and aware. You will find more peace and life will be more meaningful.

RELAX

Relaxation, meditation, and prayer help you go slow in life. Know the long-term benefits of these, but be in the present state of mind always. Slow down from the fast-paced daily routine Practice deep relaxation. In 1978, Robert Keith Wallace completed a 10-year study of meditators, evaluating their biological age via three indicators- Blood pressure, hearing, and near point vision. He found that subjects who had meditated more than five years were on average twelve years younger biologically than those who had not meditated at all - that is a sixty-year-old had forty-eight-year-old bodies. I find that when I take time to relax, meditate or pray, I feel more balanced and in control. Relaxation gives us a sense of wellbeing and other benefits like attracting people who are more at peace with themselves.

Relaxation needs to be a daily event, preferably the same time every day, preferably early mornings so that you can avoid distractions and set yourself up for the day.

Do it while you are sitting up- if you lie down, you may fall asleep.

Do it anyway, even if you have no time. The long-term benefits of relaxation are immense.

Start every day with an intention to be balanced and peaceful. There is no guarantee that you will feel the same every day, but on most days you will be good. There will be days when you have a wonderful day throughout and there will be days when you won't get past breakfast and life hits you. But with practice, you will get better and better.

GIVE YOURSELF A BREAK

You don't need to be a genius to realize that your health and feelings are affected by the subtle energies of your environment. Have you ever noticed that you can spend your whole day in a forest walking and camping and still at the end of the day while spending even half-day amidst the concrete jungle of the city drains you of your energy? This is because nature has healing vibrations and replaces our energy. It pays to go on a trip to the mountains and waterfalls and forests, we in a way reconnect to our natural self. Have you ever noticed that when you walk into certain restaurants, you feel so good and energetic while some restaurants give a very negative feeling? When a place does not feel right, just walk away. In certain cultures over the world, there is a tradition and respect for time alone. Is it then a coincidence that all great teachers like Christ, Buddha, and Mohammad all drew inspiration from solitude, and so do all their disciples. Take time out for yourself where you are away from the ringing of the phone, newspaper or a clock, or anybody to disturb your thoughts and just be yourself with your thoughts. It can be a corner place in your house or a balcony where you are alone. It is in these moments of "me time" that we discover the real WE.

GRATITUDE

When you wake up in the morning, every day, start your day with a "Thank You God" statement. You need to be thankful that you are alive. Millions don't wake up the next morning. Being alive itself is a big blessing. Suspend all judgments about your life and the people in it. Say thanks in everything.

Thank you for my family, my home, my friends, my breakfast, and thank you for another wonderful day, would be a good way to start our day. Being grateful for what we have is a great attitude to have.

Most of us grow up with the feedback that we are not ok, that the world is not ok. We soon decide that everything in our lives is not ok. That is because we see our lives through our own glass windows.

Wonder if you have heard the story of a young couple who moved into a new apartment. One morning, the woman looked out of her kitchen window and saw the neighbors' laundry drying on a line. The clothes looked dirty, really dirty. " I don't think they know how to wash clothes. They look so dirty!" said she to her husband. Maybe they use a lousy detergent, added the husband absent-mindedly, his face still buried in the newspaper.

A few days later, this happened again. Dirty-looking laundry again. Derogatory remarks about the neighbors' incompetence again.

Then one Sunday, the woman was in for a surprise. She looked out of her window and saw really clean laundry. Ah! She exclaimed "They finally learnt how to do it right. Perhaps someone taught them how to wash clothes.

Actually dear, said her husband, "I got up early this morning and cleaned our windows."

Ouch! What's true for the couple is true for all of us too. It only confirms that what behavioral scientists have maintained all along. We see things not the way they are but the way we are. Our windows-our tinted glasses significantly impact our view of the world.

We see other people through our own stained glass windows. If we are looking for faults, we find them. Just as easily as we would find good if we go looking for that. So it helps not to jump to conclusions and damn other people. It may not be them; it may be our own windows to be blamed.

This is true not just of other people, but of life itself. If you have lived with the fear of failure all your life, you tend to erect a window of risk aversion. In every opportunity, you first see the risks, the downsides, the possibility of failure. Someone else may look at the same circumstances through an image of optimism and see a huge overpowering silver lining.

A man pulled into a petrol pump on a highway. "What are the people like in the town ahead?" he asked the attendant. The attendant replied, "What were they like in the town you are coming from?" "Awful!, said the man. Rude, cold, and unfriendly" Well, said the attendant, "I am sorry but you will find that the people in the town ahead are the same."

A little while later, another car headed in the same direction pulled in. "What are people like in the town ahead?" the driver asked the attendant. "What were they like in the town you are coming from, asked the attendant." "Wonderful said the man, warm, helpful, and friendly!" "Well, said the attendant, "I am happy to say that you will find that people in the town ahead are the same."

It's always like that. It's not about them, it's about us. It's not the world, it's the window.

Change the windows through which you see others, your family, your friends, your neighbor and you will see a totally different picture. The next time you find fault with someone, pause before you proceed to damn them. Perhaps it is time to clean your windows. Always see good in everything and be grateful for them to be in your life. They are there for a reason. To teach you a lesson.

LOVE PEOPLE: UNCONDITIONALLY

If you are asked to write in ten words or less "What is the purpose of your life," what would you write. A big mansion, a big car, a million in my bank. Secretly each of us know that there is more to life than these- People come first. Caring for people is the highest cause that one can live for and strive for. We are here to love one another.

Experiments have been carried out in American hospitals where newborn babies in one group are held and stroked for ten minutes, three times a day. Babies in the second group aren't stroked. The first group gains weight at twice the rate of the second. Medical science has a long name for this kind of treatment. We don't need scientific terms- because we are talking about love.

I have encountered so many people in my life who have said to me "All I wanted in my life was for my dad to tell me he was proud of me. All I wanted was a hug from him." If we are honest, almost everything we do is an attempt to get more love. Everyone you have met in your life, everyone you cross across the street every day, is craving for love and acceptance- and some people will go to any lengths to get it.

To love people, you don't need to kiss everyone you meet or you don't have to hand out rice bowls. Love is all about judging people less. It is allowing them to wear what they want, live how they want, and be who they are without our criticism.

FORGIVE AND FORGET

"Forgiveness is the fragrance the violet sheds on the heel that has crushed it." Mark Twain.

Most of us grew thinking that we punish other people by refusing to forgive them- that is, "If I don't forgive you, you suffer." A completely wrong philosophy to live by. Actually, it is you who is having knots in the stomach and getting affected by doing that. The other person is probably not even thinking of that. Next time you are resenting someone, close your eyes and experience your feelings, your body. Making people guilty makes you miserable. The universe does not operate on guilt and blame-guilt and blame are just stuff we have made up. It is humanly possible to let go of our resentments even in the most horrific circumstances. Heartbreak, illness, loneliness, desperation...we each get our share.   But ultimately the question is whether the experience

makes us harder or softer. Pain is inevitable,
misery is a choice.

SELF LOVE

Getting comfortable with loving yourself is the
first step towards a happy life. We can't give
anyone else something we don't have. We can

never accept other people as they are, unless we are ready to accept ourselves as we are. When we are mesmerized with our own faults, we see the same in others. We look for our faults in others and then feel good about it, in the hope that it will make us feel better. And when we find them, we don't feel better.

While we concentrate on our own faults, the world will keep punishing us and we will keep punishing ourselves. We do it with ill health, poverty, and loneliness. As long as we don't like ourselves, the world won't like us. And we blame the world.

Loving yourself means forgiving yourself. It means admitting to yourself that to this point, you have lived your life the best way you know-how. Stop seeing yourself as guilty. Forget perfection and aim for improvement. Forgive yourself for your shortcomings and automatically you begin to let others off the hook for the same things. In relationships, working on yourselves works and trying to change other people doesn't.

Have you ever been sick in bed or staying inside your house for long periods and then you go out for the first time in weeks? Isn't it exhilarating just to see the sky, the trees, the people moving around, even the grass on the ground seems so refreshing. Life is suddenly richer, not because the world has changed, but because we have. Joy comes from fresh vision.

Look for beauty in everything around you and you will find more within yourself. You see people not as they are but as you are. Your experience of the world is actually you experiencing yourself. It's all about YOU.

ACRES OF DIAMOND-GO CLAIM YOURS!!

An African farmer named Ali Hafed had heard stories of fortune from other farmers. These farmers discovered diamonds on their land and became rich beyond their wildest imagination. Ali Hafed became discontented with his own life and desperately desired the same fortune. He eventually sold his farm and left his family to begin a quest for land that would lead him to riches. He searched through many lands far and wide. Eventually, as an old man, he became depressed and despondent. He threw himself into a great tidal wave to his death, never to be seen again.

The successor of his land, another farmer, one day strolled along a creek that ran through the property. He noticed a blue flash from the creek bed, knelt down, and sifted through the water until he pulled a crystal object from the mud of the creek. He wiped it off, took it home, and left it on his mantel above the fireplace, where he quickly forgot about it.

Several weeks later, a visitor stopped by the farmer and noticing the crystal on the mantle picked it up. Instantly he became excited, he was holding a diamond in his hand. The farmer protested at first and the visitor reassured him that it was indeed a diamond. That farm eventually became one of the largest diamond mines in the world. Had Ali Hafed simply known how to identify and look for diamonds, he would have had the fortune he so desperately wanted.

We are all standing among our own acres of diamonds. We need the skills and ability to recognize what a diamond looks like in its rough state. A close friend of mine likes to say "challenges beget opportunities." Or rather, we need to see the challenges around us as diamonds ready to be cut and polished.

Find your diamonds where you are. You don't need to go places to find them. You don't need to change the world to get them. You just need to look inwards, believe in hope, work hard, and be honest, and everything you have wished for in your life will come true. That's a promise!